In
1935 if you wanted to
read a good book, you needed
either a lot of money or a library card.
Cheap paperbacks were available, but their
poor production generally mirrored the quality
between the covers. One weekend that year,
Allen Lane, Managing Director of The Bodley Head,
having spent the weekend visiting Agatha Christie,
found himself on a platform at Exeter station trying to
find something to read for his journey back to London.
He was appalled by the quality of the material he had to
choose from. Everything that Allen Lane achieved from that
day until his death in 1970 was based on a passionate belief
in the existence of 'a vast reading public for *intelligent*
books at a low price'. The result of his momentous vision
was the birth not only of Penguin, but of the 'paperback
revolution'. Quality writing became available for the price of
a packet of cigarettes, literature became a mass medium
for the first time, a nation of book-borrowers became a
nation of book-buyers – and the very concept of book
publishing was changed for ever. Those founding
principles – of quality and value, with an overarching
belief in the fundamental importance of reading –
have guided everything the company has
done since 1935. Sir Allen Lane's
pioneering spirit is still very much alive
at Penguin in 2005. Here's to
the next 70 years!

MORE THAN A BUSINESS

'We decided it was time to end the almost customary half-hearted manner in which cheap editions were produced – as though the only people who could possibly want cheap editions must belong to a lower order of intelligence. We, however, believed in the existence in this country of a vast reading public for intelligent books at a low price, and staked everything on it'
Sir Allen Lane, 1902–1970

'The Penguin Books are splendid value for sixpence, so splendid that if other publishers had any sense they would combine against them and suppress them'
George Orwell

'More than a business … a national cultural asset'
Guardian

'When you look at the whole Penguin achievement you know that it constitutes, in action, one of the more democratic successes of our recent social history'
Richard Hoggart

Borneo and the Poet

REDMOND O'HANLON

PENGUIN BOOKS

PENGUIN BOOKS

Published by the Penguin Group

Penguin Books Ltd, 80 Strand, London WC2R 0RL, England
Penguin Group (USA) Inc., 375 Hudson Street, New York, New York 10014, USA
Penguin Group (Canada), 10 Alcorn Avenue, Toronto, Ontario, Canada M4V 3B2
(a division of Pearson Penguin Canada Inc.)
Penguin Ireland, 25 St Stephen's Green, Dublin 2, Ireland
(a division of Penguin Books Ltd)
Penguin Group (Australia), 250 Camberwell Road, Camberwell, Victoria 3124,
Australia (a division of Pearson Australia Group Pty Ltd)
Penguin Books India Pvt Ltd, 11 Community Centre,
Panchsheel Park, New Delhi – 110 017, India
Penguin Group (NZ), cnr Airborne and Rosedale Roads, Albany,
Auckland 1310, New Zealand (a division of Pearson New Zealand Ltd)
Penguin Books (South Africa) (Pty) Ltd, 24 Sturdee Avenue,
Rosebank 2196, South Africa

Penguin Books Ltd, Registered Offices: 80 Strand, London WC2R 0RL, England

www.penguin.com

Into the Heart of Borneo first published by The Salamander Press 1984
Published in Penguin Books 1985
This extract published as a Pocket Penguin 2005

2

Copyright © Redmond O'Hanlon, 1984
All rights reserved

The moral right of the author has been asserted

Set in 11/13pt Monotype Dante
Typeset by Palimpsest Book Production Limited
Polmont, Stirlingshire
Printed in England by Clays Ltd, St Ives plc

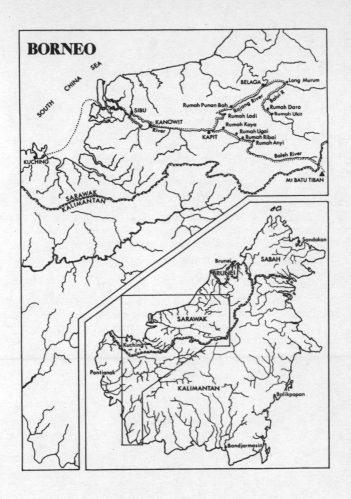

The situation in Sarawak as seen by Haddon in 1888 is still much the same today. He found a series of racial strata moving downwards in society and backwards in time as he moved inwards on the island.

C. D. Darlington, *The Evolution of Man and Society*, 1969

As a former academic and a natural-history-book reviewer I was astonished to discover, on being threatened with a two-month exile to the primary jungles of Borneo, just how fast a man can read.

Powerful as your scholarly instincts may be, there is no matching the strength of that irrational desire to find a means of keeping your head upon your shoulders; of retaining your frontal appendage in its accustomed place; of barring 1,700 different species of parasitic worm from your bloodstream and Wagler's pit viper from just about anywhere; of removing small, black, wild-boar ticks from your crutch with minimum discomfort (you do it with Sellotape); of declining to wear a globulating necklace of leeches all day long; of sidestepping amoebic and bacillary dysentery, blackwater and dengue fevers, malaria, cholera, typhoid, rabies, hepatitis, tuberculosis and the crocodile (thumbs in its eyes, if you have time, they say).

A rubber suit, with a pair of steel waders, seemed the obvious answer. But then the temperature runs to 95°F in the shade, and the humidity is 98 per cent. Hose and McDougall's great two-volume masterpiece *The Pagan Tribes of Borneo* (1912), Alfred Russel Wallace's *The Malay Archipelago: the Land of the Orang-Utan and the Bird of Paradise* (2 vols, 1869; a book even richer than its title indicates), Odoardo Beccari's *Wanderings in the Great Forests of Borneo* (1904), Hose's *The Field-book of a Jungle-Wallah* (1929) and Robert Shelford's *A Naturalist in Borneo* (1916) offered no immediate solution. And then meek, dead, outwardly unimpressive, be-suited and bowler-hatted Uncle Eggy came to my rescue.

Reading Tom Harrisson's memoirs of the war against the Japanese in Borneo, *World Within* (1959), I came across the following passage. Harrisson, sent out of his own unit on a secret mission, faces his selector:

In the relics of a Northumberland Avenue hotel, I was interviewed by Colonel Egerton-Mott . . . Mott offered me Borneo . . . adding that I was about the last of their hopes. They had already (he said) asked everyone with any conceivable knowledge of the country, including my colleagues of the 1932 Oxford expedition. When I practically leapt at the offer, he shed his cavalry veneer of calm for a second in pleased evident relief. For, in a tiny way, the British services at that moment badly needed to find a few men to go back into Borneo and try to save some of the face, chin-up, lost to the Japanese.

For the next few weeks my lately softening feet hardly felt ground. Special Operations Executive, 'SOE', the British centre of cloak-and-dagger, was a most efficient organisation, in a different class from the ordinary army or civilian services. Parachuting, coding, disguise, hiding, searching, tailing, burglaring, stealing trains, blowing up railway bridges, shamming deafness, passing on syphilis, resisting pain, firing from the hip, forgery and the interruption of mail, were some things one could learn in intense concentration. None of them would be of much use in the east. But the acquisition of so much criminal and lethal knowledge gave a kick of self-confidence.

So now, at last, I knew how my mild-mannered uncle had really spent his time, the nature of that 'something in the City' and those 'interests in the East' of which my aunt would speak with such disdain. Armed with my newly-revealed ancestor, I decided to seek help from the intellectual descendants of the Special Operations Executive.

The training area of 22 SAS near Hereford is the best place on earth from which to begin a journey upriver into the heart of the jungle. The nearest I had ever come to a tropical rain-forest, after all, was in the Bodleian Library, via the pages of the great nineteenth-century traveller-naturalists, Humboldt, Darwin,

Wallace, Bates, Thomas Belt – and, in practice, a child-hood spent rabbiting in the Wiltshire woods. My companion James Fenton, however, whose idea the venture was, enigmatic, balding, an ex-correspondent of the war in Vietnam and Cambodia, a jungle in himself, was a wise old man in these matters.

Still, as the gates swung open from a remote control point in the guardroom and our camouflaged Land Rover climbed the small track across the fields, even James was unnerved by the view. Booby-trapped lorries and burnt-out vehicles littered the landscape; displaced lines of turf disclosed wires running in all directions; from Neolithic-seeming earthworks, there came the muffled hammering of silenced small-arms fire; impossibly burly hippies in Levi jeans and trendy sweaters piled out of a truck like fragments of a hand-grenade and disappeared into the grass; mock-up streets and shuttered embassies went past, and then, as we drove round a fold in the hill, an airliner appeared, sitting neatly in a field of wheat.

'What's that?' said James.

Malcolm and Eddy forbore to reply.

We drew up by a fearsome assault course (the parallel bars you are supposed to scramble over with enthusiasm reared into the sky like a dockside crane) and made our way into the local SAS jungle. Apart from the high wire perimeter fence, the frequency with which Land Rovers drove past, the number of helicopters overhead and the speed with which persons unknown were discharging revolvers from a place whose exact position it was impossible to ascertain, it might have been a wood in England.

'What a pity,' said Malcolm, 'that you can't come to Brunei with us for a week. We could really sort you out and set you up over there.'

'What a pity,' I agreed, moistening with sweat at the very thought.

'Some people just can't hack the jungle at all,' said Eddy.

'Now,' said Malcolm, taking a small green package out of the newly-designed Bergen back-pack, 'it's all very simple. You find two trees eight feet apart where there's no evidence of any silt on the ground – the rivers can rise eighteen feet overnight and you don't want to drown in a wet dream, do you? Check the tree trunks for termites. Termites mean dead branches and dead branches, sooner or later, mean dead men. We lost a lot of men like that, in storms at night. Tie these cords round the trees, put these metal stiffeners across each end like this, and there's your hammock. If the CT [Communist Terrorists] are very good, they can pick you up by the cord marks on the bark, so brush them down in the morning. Now – here's your mossie net and you just tie it over your hammock and peg it out by these strings to the surrounding bushes until it forms a good tight box like that – and you really want to watch it, because malaria pills only give you 30 per cent protection. Here's your top cover – take some tape in case it tears round those eye-holes; mine always did after two or three months – and that's it; there's your genuine basha.'

A long green tube had materialised above the brambles in front of us, seemingly in a minute or two.

'Stop around three or four in the afternoon,' said Malcolm, 'give yourself plenty of time. Light one of these blocks that makes no smoke and boil up a cup of tea. And just sit by your tree until dark if the enemy are about. Now – who's going to test it?'

I looked hard at James.

James looked hard at a bush.

The hammock was about five feet off the ground. So this was it, the first piece of action, day one . . . Darwin, I remembered, had had excruciating problems trying to get into his hammock, but I just could not quite recall how he had solved them. I took in a great deal of air, which is how the grouper fish breaks surface, and got airborne backwards. Nets, ropes, parachute cords, canvas sheets and metal stiffener rods strung me up from throat to ankles.

'It's a good job the trees are young and fit, anyway,' said Eddy, 'or you'd have brought the whole lot down on us.'

Back at the quartermaster's stores we signed for our new kit. One Silva and one prismatic compass (black and heavy as a little bomb in its canvas belt-case); two parangs – thick knives eighteen inches long which had chopped and slashed their way through the Indonesian confrontation from 1962 to 1966;

torches; belts; pouches; powders; insect repellents; parachute cord; water bottles; water-purifying tablets; stoves; fuel blocks; mess-tins; the complete basha equipment and rations enough (Menu C) for three patrols moving in groups of four for three weeks.

It was Test Week at Hereford – the final week of the selection course during which the SAS take their pick of the eager volunteers from other regiments, and as we piled up our booty a young man with glazed eyes walked silently in, deposited his compass on the counter, and left.

'He's done well,' said Malcolm. 'No messing there. He's the first back today. Forty-five miles over the Beacons. Fifty-pound Bergen. Twelve-pound belt kit. Eighteen-pound rifle. If you add in the hills it works out at three marathons on the trot, so they say.' I was glad we were merely going to the jungle.

'Good luck lads,' said Malcolm, sending us off to see the Major in charge of the Training Wing. 'We've left a lot of men in Borneo – know what I mean?'

The soft-spoken Major, veteran of Special Forces campaigns in occupied Europe in the Second World War, of the war in Malaya, of Jebel Akhdar, Aden, Borneo and Dhofar, was huge. It was vastly reassuring to think that so much muscle could actually squeeze itself into a jungle and come out again undiminished. And his office, hung with battle honours, Special Air Service shields emblazoned with the Regiment's motto, *Qui ose gagne*; with a mass of wall charts documenting the progress of

his latest candidates; with cartoons of all the wrong
ways to resist interrogation; and libraried with strictly
practical works in natural history – on edible fungi,
on traps and tracking and poaching, on different
recipes for the cooking of rats and instructions on
the peeling of cockroaches – was an impressive place.
Determined young men stared down on us from the
line of group photographs of each year's successful
applicants. Several of them, I noticed, had two diag-
onal lines drawn across their bodies with a felt-tip
pen. In just one helicopter crash in the Falklands
eighteen men had been drowned: the regiment's
largest single loss since 1945.

'You'll find the high spot of your day,' said the
Major, 'is cleaning your teeth. The only bit of you
you can keep clean. Don't shave in the jungle, because
the slightest nick turns septic at once. And don't take
more than one change of clothes, because you must
keep your Bergen weight well down below sixty
pounds. And don't expect your Iban trackers to carry
it for you, either, because they have enough to do
transporting their own food. So keep one set of dry
kit in a sealed bag in your pack. Get into that each
night after you've eaten. Powder yourself all over,
too, with zinc talc – don't feel sissy about it – you'll
halve the rashes and the rot and the skin fungus.
Then sleep. Then get up at five thirty and into your
wet kit. It's uncomfortable at first, but don't weaken
– ever; if you do, there'll be two sets of wet kit in
no time, you'll lose sleep and lose strength and then

8

there'll be a disaster. But take as many dry socks as you can. Stuff them into all the crannies in your pack. And, in the morning, soak the pairs you are going to wear in Autan insect repellent, to keep the leeches out of your boots. Stick it on your arms and round your waist and neck and in your hair while you're about it, but not on your forehead because the sweat carries it into your eyes and it stings. Cover yourself at night, too, against the mosquitoes. Take them seriously, because malaria is a terrible thing and it's easy to get, pills or no.

'Get some jungle boots, good thick trousers and strong shirts. You won't want to nancy about in shorts once the first leech has had a go at you, believe me. Acclimatise slowly. The tropics takes people in different ways. Fit young men may pass out top here and then just collapse in Brunei. You'll think it's the end of the world. You can't breathe. You can't move. And then after two weeks you'll be used to it. And once in the jungle proper you'll never want to come out.

'It's a beautiful country and the Iban are a fine people. I was on the Baram myself, but to go up the Rajang and the Baleh will be better for your purposes. That's a good plan. The Baleh is very seldom visited, if at all, upriver, and the Tiban mountains should be very wild indeed. They look small on a map, those mountains, but they're tough going. One steep hill after another. And you have to be good with a compass. Any questions? No. Good. Well done, lads, Goodbye and good luck.'

James and I drove out past the guardroom and the police post in a stunned silence, the back of the car bristling with serious, dark-green and camouflage-brown equipment; and we fell into the King's Arms. Some hours later we found ourselves in the cathedral, mutely surveying the Mappa Mundi, drawn on vellum by Richard of Haldingham *c*.1300. Jerusalem was there all right, plum in the centre; Borneo was nowhere to be seen; but its inhabitants, for all we and Richard of Haldingham knew, had strayed across his big brown chart of the earth; there they were: the *Philli* ('test the chastity of their wives by exposing their new-born children to serpents'), the *Phanesii* ('are covered with the skin of their ears. A bat-like people with enormous drooping ears') and the *Essendones* ('it is their custom to carry out the funeral of their parents with singing and collecting a company of friends to devour the actual corpses with their teeth'). Was it time to stay at home?

*   *   *

At dawn the jungle was half-obscured in a heavy morning mist; and through the cloudy layers of rising moisture came the whooping call, the owl-like, clear, ringing hoot of the female Borneo gibbon.

Replacing the dry socks, pants, trousers and shirt inside two plastic bags inside the damp Bergen, tying them tightly to keep out the ants, I shook the wet clothes. A double-barrelled charge of insects propelled itself from inside my trouser-legs. I groomed my pants free of visible bugs, covered myself in SAS anti-fungus powder until my erogenous zone looked like meat chunks rolled in flour, ready for the heat, and forced my way into clammy battle-dress for the day. It was a nasty five o'clock start; but in half an hour the mist would be gone, the sun merciless, and the river-water soaking one anyway.

Every bush seemed to hold an unseen bird, all in full throat. There were blackbird and thrush, nightingale and warbler-like notes from every side, but more urgent and powerful and relentless, the fortissimo calls of babblers and trillers and bulbuls.

After a breakfast of fish and rice, we re-packed the dugout and set off upriver. The gibbons, having proclaimed the boundaries of their territories, ceased calling. The world changed colour from a dark watery blue to mauve to sepia to pink and then the sun rose, extraordinarily fast.

Inghai put on his peaked cap to shield his eyes from the sun as he sat on the bow and scanned the turbulent water ahead for rocks and logs; Dana, in chiefly style, wore his round hat, as large and intricately patterned as a gaming table; and Leon, proudly switching his outboard to full power, wore a mutant hybrid of pork-pie and homberg. James adjusted his boater, stretched out his legs on his half of the duckboards, and addressed himself to Swift.

Something large and flappy was crossing the river in front of us. Was it a bird disguised as a leaf-skeleton? Was it a day-flying bat disguised as a hair-net? Or was a lattice of tropical worms in transit across my retina?

Very slowly, unconcerned, the something made its floating and dipping, floating and dipping, indecisive flight right over the boat: it was an odd idea indeed, *Hestia idea*, a butterfly with grey and white wings like transparent gauze, highly poisonous, and safe from predators. In one of the richest of tropical rain forests, in a natural zone which actually contains more kinds of butterflies and moths than all other habitats of the world put together, it was ridiculously pleasing to have identified just one more species, even if, as I eventually had to admit to James, it was the most immediately obvious of them all.

James, momentarily, re-directed his critical gaze from Swift's sometimes-defective scansion, and fixed it upon the surrounding jungle. With A1 vision in both eyes which are set so far apart that he does, in this one respect, resemble a hammer-head shark, he announced, in a statement which later became formulaic and, for the Iban (and, well, just a little, for me), the incantation of a shaman of immeasurable age and wisdom summoning the spirits of the forest to dance before him: 'Redmond, I am about to see something *marvellous*.'

The canoe swung into the next bend and there, majestically perched upon a dead branch across an inlet, was a Crested serpent eagle.

'How's that?' said James.

The eagle was thick-set, black and brown and grey, his stomach lightly freckled, his head plumed flat.

James was sitting up, boatered, bearded-black, his shirt dazzling white. James looked at the eagle. The eagle looked at James. The eagle, deciding that it was too early in the morning to hallucinate, flapped off into the jungle, puzzled.

Gradually, the rapids became more frequent, more difficult to scale. Leon would align the boat carefully in the deep pools beneath each one, open up to full throttle on a straight run, shut off the engine, cock the propeller well up out of the water as we hit the first curve of white foam, grab his pole as Inghai and Dana snatched up theirs, and then all three would punt the canoe up, in wild rhythm with each other.

They were lean, fit, strong with a lifetime of unremitting exercise, their muscles flexing and bunching, etched out as clearly as Jan van Calcar's illustrations to *De humani corporis fabrica*. But we were about to discover the one disadvantage in their fondly mistaken idea of ourselves, the present misconception in the ancient myth of their oral tradition, that the ancestors of their race had been white, and giants, as strong and courageous, as all-powerful as we, too, must be.

The solid tree-trunk keel of the hollowed-out canoe began to thud against the boulders beneath the cascades of water, lightly at first, and then with alarming violence as the day wore on. We had to jump out beneath each rapid, take the long bow-rope, walk up the stones strewn down beside the fall, wade into the deep current above and pull, guiding the bow up. The water pushed irregularly at our waist and knees, sometimes embracing us like a succubus might (after a year in prison), sometimes trying a flowing rugby tackle, sometimes holding our ankles in a hydrolastic gin-trap, but never entirely friendly. With nothing but locked spines and clamped cartilages we leant back against the great flow of water on its way to the South China Sea, against the forward pull of the rope; itself tugging and slackening as the poled boat broke free or stuck fast.

Just in time, by a deep pool, in a harbour formed by two massive fallen hardwoods, Dana ruled that it was noon and we were hungry. The boat was tied up, we collapsed, and Leon went fishing.

Spreading our wet clothes out on the burning hot boulders, James and I took a swim and a wash. The clear shallows were speckled with little fish, darting shoals of orange and silver, weaving flocks of black and red; there were dull-coloured tiddlers, minnow-like, and bright fish with streamers, their small fins fanning in the current; they gathered round our feet, fixed our toes with their tiny eyes, chased whirling flecks of soap in the current.

Dana, intrigued by medicated Vosene, shampooed his glossy black hair and then rinsed it by swimming very fast across the pool underwater, a moving V of ripples on the surface marking his passage through the spins and eddies. Wading ashore, even his dark-blue tattoos glistened in the sun. Covered in circles and rosettes, whorls and lines (soot from a cooking pot, mixed with sweetened water, and punched into the skin with a bamboo stick and small hammer) the large tattoo on his throat (the most painful of all to suffer, and the most likely to produce septicaemia) testified to his immediate courage; on his thighs an intricate pattern of stylised Rhinoceros hornbill heads bespoke his chiefly status; and on the top joints of his fingers a series of dots and cross-hatchings suggested that he had taken heads in battle, probably from the bodies of invading Indonesian soldiers killed in the 1962–66 confrontation by the SAS, with whom he had sometimes served as a tracker. Dignified, intelligent, full of natural authority, at forty an old man in the eyes of his tribe, he was the law-giver and judge of conduct, the arbiter of when to plant and when to harvest the padi, and, perhaps most important of all, the chief augurer to his people, the interpreter of the messengers of the gods, the birds.

He regarded us with protective amusement. We were like the white men he had met in the war, Leon had informed us in hushed tones; we had stayed in his longhouse and behaved like guests he could trust, not offending against custom, well-mannered. James and I, in turn, decided that Tuai Rumah Dana, Lord of the House, a Beowulf, or, more accurately, a warrior-king out of Homer, was a great improvement on all our previous headmasters, deans and wardens.

Leon surfaced by the far bank of the river, half-obscured by the roots of a giant tree which twisted into the water, but obviously excited, ferociously excited. He was yelling wildly in Iban to Dana and Inghai, 'Labi-labi!' holding his harpoon cord with both hands; and, to us, 'Fish! Round fish! Big round fish!'

Dana and Inghai leapt into the dugout and put off fast across the current. It seemed a lot of fuss about a fish, however big and round.

Dana cut two lengths of our parachute cord, one for himself and one for Inghai and, tying the boat to a branch, plunged in. Something thrashed and splashed, churning up the water between the three of them. Lowering the cord, knotted into a noose, Dana pulled it tight, secured it to the stern of the dugout; and then all three paddled back, towing something. The boat beached, they hauled on the parachute cord. Gradually, a shiny olive dome broke surface, almost round, and about three feet across. Two pairs of webbed, thick claws were thrusting against the water, front and back. Pulling it ashore in reverse, the Iban cut two holes at the rear of its carapace and threaded a lead of rattan through each slit. It was a large Mud turtle, *Trionyx cartilagineus*, one of whose specific characteristics, described by a so-called closet-naturalist in the nineteenth-century British Museum from trophies in the collection, had been, as Wallace liked to point out, these very same restraining holes at the back of the shell.

Left alone for a moment, the turtle's head began

to emerge from a close-fitting sleeve, from folds of telescopic muscle. It had a flexible snout for a nose, a leathery green trunk; and a sad, watery eye. Dana's parang came down with great violence, missing the head, glancing off the cartilaginous armour, bucking the turtle, throwing up water and pebbles. The head retracted. Dana crouched, waiting. Some ten minutes later, the turtle once more began to look cautiously for its escape. Out came the head, inch by inch. With one blow, Dana severed the neck. The head rolled, quizzically, a little way across the sand.

After a lunch of rice and sebarau, Dana and Leon heaved the turtle on to its back, slit open its white belly, and threw its guts to the fish. The meat was cut into strips, salted, and stowed away in a basket on the boat. The empty shell, the blood drying, we left on the shingle.

The river twisted and turned and grew narrower and the great creepers, tumbling down in profusion from two hundred feet above our heads, edged closer. Every now and then we would pass a tangle of river-rubbish, leaves and sticks and dead ferns, seemingly caught in the lianas by floodwater some forty feet above the present water-level. So why did the high banks not show more sign of recent devastation? Idly watching one such clump as Leon arced the boat close to the bank before making a run up a rapid, we solved the mystery. A dumpy bird, thrush-sized, its blue and yellow beak framed by whiskers, black on its back, scarlet on its stomach, popped out of a side opening: the suspended bunches of debris were the nests of the Black-and-red broadbill.

The rapids and cascades became more frequent. We had to jump out into the river more often, sometimes to our waists, sometimes to our armpits, guiding the dugout into a side channel away from the main crash of the water through the central rocks, pushing it up the shallows.

'Saytu, dua, tiga – bata!' sang Dana, which even we could reconstruct as one, two, three, and push.

The Iban gripped the round, algae-covered stones on the river-bed easily with their muscled, calloused, spatulate toes. Our boots slipped into crevices, slithered away in the current, threatened to break off a leg at the ankle or the knee. It was only really possible to push hard when the boat was still, stuck fast, and then Headmaster Dana would shout 'Badas!' 'Well done!' But the most welcome cry became 'Npan! Npan!', an invitation to get back in, quick.

Crossing one such deep pool, collapsed in the boat, the engine re-started, we found ourselves staring at a gigantic Bearded pig sitting quietly on his haunches on the bank. Completely white, an old and lonely male, he looked at us with his piggy eyes. Dana, throwing his pole into the boat, snatched up his shotgun; Leon, abandoning the rudder, followed suit. Inghai shouted a warning, the canoe veered sideways into the current, the shotguns were discarded, the boat re-aligned, and the pig, no longer curious, ambled off into the jungle, his enormous testicles swaying along behind him.

We entered a wide reach of foaming water. The choppy waves, snatching this way and that, had ripped caves of soil out of the banks, leaving hundreds of yards of overhang on either side. There was an ominous noise of arguing currents ahead. The rapids-preamble, the white water, the moving whirlpools, the noise ahead, was longer and louder than it ought to have been.

With the canoe pitching feverishly, we rounded a sweeping bend; and the reason for the agitated river, the unaccustomed roar, became obvious. The Green Heave ahead was very much higher than any we had met. There was a waterfall to the left of the river-course, a huge surging of water over a ledge, with the way to the right blocked by thrown-up trees, piles of roots dislodged upstream, torn out in floods, and tossed aside here against a line of rocks. There was, however, one small channel through, a shallow rapid, dangerously close to the main rush of water, but negotiable, separated from the torrent by three huge boulders.

Keeping well clear of the great whirlpool beneath the waterfall, Leon, guided between rocks by Inghai's semaphore-like gestures, brought the boat to the base of this normal-size rapid. Dana, James and I made our way carefully up with the bow-rope, whilst Leon and Inghai held the dugout steady.

Dana held the lead position on the rope; I stood

behind him and James behind me. We pulled, Leon and Inghai pushed. The boat moved up and forward some fifteen feet and then stuck. Leon and Inghai walked up the rapid, kneeling, hunching and shoving, rolling small rocks aside to clear a channel. We waited on the lip of the rock above, pulling on the rope to keep the longboat straight, to stop it rolling sideways, tiring in the push of water round our waists. At last Leon and Inghai were ready. But the channel they had had to make was a little to our right as we looked down at them, a little to their left, a little closer to the waterfall. To pull straight we must move to our right. Dana pointed to our new positions.

It was only a stride or two. But the level of the river-bed suddenly dipped, long since scooped away by the pull of the main current. James lost his footing, and, trying to save himself, let go of the rope. I stepped back and across to catch him, the rope bound round my left wrist, snatching his left hand in my right. His legs thudded into mine, tangled, and then swung free, into the current, weightless, as if a part of him had been knocked into outer space. His hat came off, hurtled past his shoes, spun in an eddy, and disappeared over the lip of the fall.

His fingers were very white; and slippery. He bites his fingernails; and they could not dig into my palm. He simply looked surprised; his head seemed a long way from me. He was feeling underwater with his free arm, impossibly trying to grip a boulder with his other hand, to get a purchase on a smooth and slimy rock, a rock polished smooth, for centuries, by perpetual tons of rolling water.

His fingers bent straighter, slowly edging out of mine, for hour upon hour, or so it felt, but it must have been in seconds. His arm rigid, his fingertips squeezed out of my fist. He turned in the current, spread-eagled. Still turning, but much faster, he was sucked under; his right ankle and shoe were bizarrely visible above the surface; he was lifted slightly, a bundle of clothes, of no discernible shape, and then he was gone.

'Boat! Boat!' shouted Dana, dropping the rope, bounding down the rocks of the side rapid, crouched, using his arms like a baboon.

'Hold the boat! Hold the boat!' yelled Leon.

James's bald head, white and fragile as an owl's egg, was sweeping round in the whirlpool below, spinning, bobbing up and down in the foaming water, each orbit of the current carrying him within inches of the black rocks at its edge.

Leon jumped into the boat, clambered on to the raised outboard-motor frame, squatted, and then, with a long, yodelling cry, launched himself in a great curving leap into the centre of the maelstrom. He disappeared, surfaced, shook his head, spotted James, dived again, and caught him. Inghai, too, was in the water, but, closing with them for a moment, he faltered, was overwhelmed, and swept downstream. Leon, holding on to James, made a circuit of the whirlpool until, reaching the exit current, he thrust out like a turtle and they followed Inghai downriver, edging, yard by yard, towards the bank.

Obeying Dana's every sign, I helped him coax the boat on to a strip of shingle beneath the dam of logs. James, when we walked down to him, was sitting on a boulder. Leon sat beside him, an arm around his shoulders.

'You be all right soon, my friend,' said Leon, 'you be all right soon, my very best friend. Soon you be so happy.'

James, bedraggled, looking very sick, his white lips an open O in his black beard, was hyper-ventilating dangerously, taking great rhythmic draughts of oxygen, his body shaking.

'You be okay,' said Leon. 'I not let you die, my old friend.'

Just then little Inghai appeared, beaming with pride, holding aloft one very wet straw boater.

'I save hat!' said Inghai. 'Jams! Jams! I save hat!'

James looked up, smiled, and so stopped his terrible spasms of breathing. He really was going to be all right.

Suddenly, it all seemed funny, hilariously funny. 'Inghai saved his hat!' We laughed and laughed, rolling about on the shingle. 'Inghai saved his hat! Ingy-pingy saved his hat!' It was, I am ashamed to say, the first (and I hope it will be the last) fit of genuine medically-certifiable hysterics which I have ever had.

*

Dana, looking at James, decided that we would camp where we were. Finding a level plateau way above flood level on the bank behind us, the pole hut and the pole beds were soon built. I had a soap and a swim, re-covered myself in SAS super-strength insect repellent and silky crutch powder, re-filled our water bottles from the river and dosed each one with water-purifying pills, took a handful of vitamin pills myself, forced James and the Iban to take their daily meas-ure, too, and then settled down against a boulder with my pipe (to further discourage mosquitoes), a mess-mug full of arak, and the third edition of Smythies's *The Birds of Borneo*.

James, covered in butterflies, was reading *Les Misérables* and looking a little miserable himself.

'How are you feeling?'

'Not too good, Redmond. I get these palpitations at the best of times. I've had attacks ever since Oxford. I take some special pills for it but they're really not much help. In fact the only cure is to rest a bit and then be violently sick as soon as possible.'

'Can I do anything?'

'No,' said James, pulling on his umpteenth ciga-rette and concentrating on Victor Hugo.

He was, I decided, an even braver old wreck than I had imagined. Looking fondly at his great bald head I was really fairly pleased with Leon for helping the future of English literature; for preventing the disarrangement of all those brain cells; for denying all those thousands of brightly-coloured little fish in the shallows the chance to nibble at torn fragments of cerebellar tissue, to ingest synapses across which had once run electrical impulses carrying stored memories of a detailed knowledge of literature in Greek and Latin, in German and French, in Spanish and Italian. But all the same, I wondered, what would we do if an accident befell us in the far interior, weeks away from any hospital, beyond the source of the Baleh, marching through the jungle towards the Tiban range and well away, even, from the stores in the boat?

Dana took his single-barrelled shotgun, held together with wire and strips of rattan, and set off to find a wild pig. Leon and Inghai went fishing with their harpoons. My Balkan Sobranie tobacco, as ninety-per-cent humid as everything else, tasted as rich and wet as a good gravy, and the more arak I had, the less like fermented elastoplast it became. And it actually made one see things.

A long white strip of silk chiffon detached itself from the tumultuous green tumble of trees and creepers on the opposite bank and undulated, as slowly as a lamprey in a lake, diagonally downstream. It was a very feminine apparition, redolent of everything I was beginning to miss, of silky rustles, lacy white knickers, of mysteriously intricate suspenders, of long, soft, white silk stockings dropped beside the bed. I looked at the arak with increased respect, and took some more.

A question framed itself, with great deliberation.

What if, just supposing for a moment, it was not a suspender belt, but a butterfly? There were weirder things in the air in Borneo than suspender belts, after all. There was, for instance, and I planned to see it near Mount Tiban, an owl, *Glaucidium borneense*, 'about the size of one's thumb', as Hose described it, which calls poop-te-poop-poop; 'and also a tiny hawk, *Microhierax*, which lays a large white egg about as big as itself'. Birds of the high montane moss forests, they 'settle on the dead trees; and as these are of a notable height, they look like insects, being in fact very much smaller than some of the large butterflies'.

In fact – perhaps it was a bird? Maybe I could identify it in Smythies without leaving my increasingly comfortable boulder to rummage for the small library in my Bergen, Home of the Ant? There it was – unmistakable, the male Paradise flycatcher, trailing two white tail feathers, each eighteen inches long. Its call is '*auk auk* very like that of a frog (Banks). One of the loudest calls in the forest – both sexes call (Harrisson).' So it was a bird that looked like a butterfly, flew like a suspender belt, and sang like a frog. I fell into a deep sleep.

Leon woke me up for supper, handing me a mess-tin of sebarau and rice. Dana returned, his legs running with blood.

'What the hell's happened to him, Leon?'

'It's nothing! That's – how you say it? Leeches?'

Dana washed his legs in the river and joined us

round Inghai's fire. He handed me a couple of cartridges, gesticulating angrily. The fulminite caps had been banged in by the firing pin, but the tube was still crimped, the main charge of powder un-exploded. I laid them gingerly under a rock.

'They must have got wet.'

'No,' said Leon. 'Dana says Malay cartridges, Chinese cartridges, no good. English cartridges always go off, boom! He creep up on two pigs. Click. Nothing at all. He put in another. Click. The pigs hear him. Foof. They run away. So no babi. No roast babi in a pot. Only fishes stew.'

'Leon,' I said, 'why did you cry like that, when you saved James's life?'

'Well,' said Leon, shuffling his bare feet on the sand, 'we Christians like you, of course, but, all the same, we respect the river. The river like Jams. The river take Jams away. So we say sorries to the river, because we take him back again.'

James was picking at his bony fish in the mess-tin, pushing his rice aside.

'Excuse me,' he said, got up, lurched a little, and was horribly sick into a bush.

'Now you better, my best friend,' said Leon, 'now I give you more rices. Makai! Eat up! Makai, Jams!'

The sky grew black suddenly. There was an odd breeze. Everyone – insects, monkeys, birds, frogs – stopped making a noise. Dana, Leon and Inghai ran to the dugout, dragged it high up the shingle and re-tied it, bow and stern, with long ropes leading to trees on the high bank. Huge globules of water began to fall, splashing star-burst patterns on the dry hot rocks along the shore. We made for the bashas, changed fast, and slipped inside. Rain splattered on the tree canopy two hundred feet above, a whispery noise growing duller and increasing in volume to a low drumming. Drops hit our canvas awnings and bounced off; a fine spray came sideways through the mosquito net. A wind arrived; and we heard the first tree start its long crashing fall far off in the forest. Thunder rumbled nearer, and, every few seconds, the trunks of the trees immediately in view through the triangular gap at the foot of the basha were bright with lightning flashes, reflected power from balls and sheets and zig-zags of light, energy that lit the clumps of lichen on the bark with startling clarity, that picked out the tendrils of fungus and the stalks of spore-bodies like heads of unkempt hair.

I fell asleep and I dreamed of James's sister Chotty. She was coming at me with a particular knife she uses to make her beef stews, her pheasant pies. 'It's quite all right,' she said. 'It doesn't matter now that he's drowned. There's no need to apologise. I don't want to hear your explanations.'

* * *

In the morning, the world was soaked, the mist was thick, and the river had risen five or six feet. After a breakfast of rice and fish, James and I walked ahead up the steeply sloping bank and Dana and Leon and Inghai easily brought the boat up the now-deeper side rapid. The water was full of broken branches, old logs which had broken free from their previous snags, ferns, lengths of creeper, and mud. A dead green bird like a parakeet, perhaps a Green broad-bill, floated past.

Dana confined James to the boat, or else put us ashore beneath a rapid, making us walk up and round it and picking us up beside the pools above; but in any case the temporary change in water-level made the going easier, submerging some cataracts alto-gether, filling channels through others. We had almost grown accustomed to the kingfishers, the herons, the fish-eagles that escorted us ahead. But there was one bird that always puzzled me, a new concept in eagles, occasionally wheeling over us, screaming its shrill cry, repeating it again and again. Sometimes it made this call and it was black; some-times it made the same call and it was white, and barred-brown under the wings. One of them might have been Blyth's Hawk eagle, but for the cry. Probably, as Smythies told us, it was the Changeable hawk eagle, an odd species in which, in part-defiance of Darwin's rules for the mechanism of sexual selection, the two different plumages are haphazardly distrib-uted with no apparent regard for male or female, age or range.

We made good progress, twisting and turning and rising up the narrowing river for mile upon mile. At one point, where the river split into two around an island, the trees on either bank were so close together that their branches touched and, over our heads, a troop of Pig-tailed macaques, on all fours, their tails slightly curled and held up in the air behind them, like those of so many cats pleased to be home, were making an aerial crossing. They scrutinised us for a moment or two, and then scampered for cover.

Further up, in a massively-buttressed oak-like tree, sat something large and furry, a rich, mahogany red back and side of fur with its head obscured by leaves. Just for a moment, I thought it might be an orang-utan, but had to admit that it was scarcely probable; we were far more likely to have caught a glimpse of a Maroon leaf monkey, Hose's Maroon langur.

In any case, it was just then that James promised to see something marvellous, having, I believe, seen it already. High up, circling in a sky which at that time of day can look almost English, heat-wave, August-blue with a fluff of clouds, were two enormous eagles, pitch-black, their tails surprisingly long: Black eagles.

The river became shallower as the day wore on and once again I had to push the boat, almost continuously. It was shattering work, heaving against the current, falling over the stones on the river-bed. The Iban were as fit as men could be, but an extra source of energy fuelled them, too; could it simply be the rice they ate, at each meal, some twelve times more than us, some twelve times more than one would have thought possible? I resolved to mimic Leon's diet in every particular.

At lunch-time, Leon harpooned a river tortoise, about eighteen inches long with a muddy black cara-pace and its plastron flat and blotched with yellow and black. He was stowed, sadly, beneath the duck-boards of the dugout. Inghai caught yet more seba-rau, and we roasted them over an open fire. Expecting to keel over like a blown bull at any moment, to explode disgustingly amongst the rocks, I forced myself to eat as much sticky, finger-gluing rice as Leon did, to the great approval of the Iban and the horror of the Fenton. Life began to seem even better, and much rounder.

* * *

The next day the river became more difficult still: an unending series of rapids and snags and boulders. The dugout seemed to increase its weight with every mile; the 120° heat, bearing down and beating off the surface of the water, seemed less easy to struggle through, even when the warm water was up to one's neck. Two towels bound round my head failed to keep the sweat out of my eyes and off my glasses.

There were fewer laughs at lunch-time on the shingle. The river was too low, said Dana, the going too tough. We now needed two small canoes instead of one big one. Only Leon, immensely strong, cheer-ful and affectionate, was undaunted. He was obviously a champion river-hunter, too: while we lay, exhausted, in the shade of a jungle chestnut tree, he disappeared, swimming underwater up an adjacent creek. Half an hour later he returned, towing a fresh trophy. It was much longer than he was: a big Water monitor, a black and yellow prehistoric dragon with a long forked tongue which it protruded like a snake. Dana and Leon pulled it up the bank. It stood four-square, clear of the ground, hissing, and lashing its long tail, the harpoon stuck through its side. Dana drew his parang and killed it with a blow to the head.

The lizard strapped into the dugout, we set off again. It was too arduous to notice much – for hour upon hour I was only really conscious of the whirling water, the side of the boat and my own gripping positions on the gunwale. But then the country began to open out, the big trees stepped back from the bank; rolling hills, covered with nothing but young scrub-jungle, stretched away to a forest horizon. The Iban looked about them uneasily. There was no mark of all this on our secret government maps.

We continued on our way for a mile or so and then, glancing up, I found myself looking into the big brown eyes of a girl on the bank beside us. She was standing in a loose clump of bamboo, her fine black hair falling over her bare shoulders and breasts.

'Kayan?' shouted Dana.

The girl turned and fled.

A little further on, four men, in two small canoes, were setting nets.

'Kayan?' Dana repeated.

'Kenyah!' shouted the men, much insulted. They yelled instructions above the noise of the water, pointing upriver.

'Can you understand them, Leon?'

'No,' said Leon, uncharacteristically quiet. 'These are not our peoples.'

The river meandered, grew broader and more shallow, and then entered a very long straight reach. A paradise was disclosed. An inland kingdom, secluded almost beyond reach, of padi fields and banana trees, palms and coconuts, lay in its own wide valley, surrounded by jungle hills; a huge longhouse, its atap roof blending into the landscape, was set back from the left bank of the river, about three miles off; some forest giants had been left standing, here and there, and on one of these a pair of Brahminy kites were sitting, the birds of Singalang Burong, King of the Gods.

Cheered by amused men in light fishing canoes and by families from their farms on the banks, it took us two hours to manhandle the heavy dugout up to the beach beneath the longhouse.

About to wade ashore, Dana stopped me emphatically, pointing me to my place on the duckboards.

'We must waits,' said Leon. 'This not our country.'

About sixty children watched us silently from the bank. Some of their mothers, their ear-lobes, weighted by brass rings, dangling down below their shoulders, watched too. In about a quarter of an hour, after much to-ing and fro-ing, the chief's son arrived and formally invited us to set foot on his tribal lands.

Heaving the Bergens on to our backs we followed

him towards the longhouse along a network of paths laid out between the padi stores, huts on stilts, each with its own ladder and with a close-fitting down-turned plate of wood set around each stilt to keep out the rats. The settlement was obviously large and well-organised. Even the dogs looked young and healthy. And the longhouse, when we reached it, was spectacular. Massively constructed on tree-trunk piles and a forest of lesser stilts, it was about three hundred yards long, the main floor set fifteen feet from the ground. Dark, hairy, boar-like pigs, indistinguishable from the Wild bearded pigs of the jungle, rooted and grunted amongst the garbage between the poles; chickens, the cockerels looking as magnificent as the ancestral Jungle fowl, scratched about amongst the pigs, and favourite dogs, stretched out on the side of the verandah, lolled their heads over the edge of the bamboo platform and observed our arrival with mild interest.

Climbing a slippery notched log up to a longhouse with a sixty-pound Bergen on one's back is not easy, and I went up the muddy trunk almost on all fours, holding on hard with both hands. The Iban and the chief's son paused while James and I took our shoes off; we then crossed the outer apron and the roofed verandah and were ushered into the chief's quarters. The room stretched, at right angles, back from the line of the longhouse for about a hundred feet. It was cross-beamed and triangularly roofed like a barn, the huge timbers cross-cut into one another and

lashed with rattan. There were several sleeping plat-
forms, some with curtains, some with bamboo parti-
tions round them, down one side of the room. The
chief's son, smaller, fairer-skinned than the Iban, but
just as muscular and just as dignified, indicated a
patch of floor where we might sleep. Dana and he,
to their mutual delight, began to talk, albeit with no
great fluency.

'They very clever mens,' said Leon, 'they both talk
Kayan.'

'Can you talk Kayan?'

Leon grinned.

'Only very dirty words. A girl she told them to
me. A very silly Kayan girls. But I talk English.'

'Well, you'll have to translate *everything*. You'll
have to help us – you ask Dana what they're saying.'

Leon and Dana talked rapidly in Iban.

'The son of the chief says he very sorries. Almost
all the people are in the fields, but they come back
tonight. The chief is away on the Mahakam.'

'The Mahakam?'

'These people they come from there. They come
fifteen years ago. This good land, very good.'

So they had crossed over the mountains from the
great Mahakam basin, from Indonesia, from the river
that flowed south-east, into the Makassar Strait.

'We have fun tonight,' said Leon.

I awoke instantly from a passing reverie, a reali-
sation that we must be within striking distance of the
centre of Borneo, perhaps almost within reach of the

wild, nomadic, primitive peoples, the Ukit, the men who could tell us, if anyone could, whether or no the Borneo rhinoceros was still to be found.

'Hey Leon,' I said, a little too anxiously, 'step outside a minute, will you? I've something very important to tell you.'

'Eh?'

'Come on.'

Out on the verandah, I grabbed his tattooed arm. 'Look – don't tell James, because he wouldn't like it, he's so modest. But, in England, he's *very* famous. He is the poet of all the tribe, the chief poet in all England. His *whole life* is making songs. That's what he does all day. You understand? He *sings songs*. And he dances. He knows *all* the dances.'

Leon was genuinely excited, immensely impressed.

'So look Leon, between now and tonight, tell everyone – or else James will just sit there – you tell everyone, via Dana, that James is the greatest poet in all England and that when it's our turn to dance and sing, they must shout for James. Okay? Will you do that?'

'He very great man,' said Leon, 'very old. Very serious man. I tell Dana.'

We began to unpack; and a crowd started to gather. The oldest woman I had yet seen in Borneo, squatting on the floor, her wrinkled breasts, and her ear-lobes, hanging forlornly, her attitude one of exaggerated distress, was alternately touching my leg and theatrically placing her hands over her eyes. I assumed that, sensibly enough, she found the sight of me painful beyond endurance and wanted this white tramp out of her drawing-room, fast. After all, with a half-grown beard, river-and-sweat-soaked shirt, water-frayed trousers and socks, and already inescapably possessed of the sweet, fetid, rotting smell of the jungle, I was even less of a truffle for the senses than usual. But I suddenly realised that she was asking for help. Her old eyes were blood-shot, her eyelids swollen. Feeling useful and needed, I pulled out my medicine pack and found the anti-biotic eye drops. Smiling broadly she disclosed her gums. Not a tooth to be seen. I squeezed in some drops and she clapped her hands.

A mother pressed forward, holding up her baby's arm. There was an angry red mound of infection on it, just below the shoulder-joint. Perhaps this was the ringworm that Harrisson wrote about.

'Kurap?' I asked.

She nodded, impatiently. I put Savlon and a dress-ing on the wound, covering up the skin which was split like a rotten tomato, and weeping like one. A queue of mothers and children formed; we dressed hundreds of cuts that had gone septic, small ulcers, patches of skin fungus, rashes. And then the men began to trickle in. They mimed, with a suppleness, a balletic grace that would have impressed Nijinsky, excruciating, disabling back pain; with eyes as big and bright as those of a fox hunting in the dusk they indicated that they were suffering from the kind of headaches that amount to concussion; with contortions that would have torn Houdini into spare ribs they demonstrated that their stomachs had ceased to function, that they were debilitated almost beyond assistance.

'Multivite,' I announced, with great solemnity.

'Alka-seltzer,' said James, as one who practised it.

I put two bright orange pills in each extended palm. Some swallowed. Some chewed. Everyone looked happy.

The eight tablets, as white and round and efficacious as sacred slices of pig tusk, sat in the bottom of James's mess-tin. Gurgle, gurgle went his upturned water bottle, and the roundels spun and bubbled and talked to each other and grew as thin as excised circles of feather cut from the very tip of the tail of the hornbill. Throwing up spray, foaming like the river in a rapid, the water rose up in the tin. The Kenyah crowded round tight, and looked in.

'Drink,' said James, handing it to the first man and staring at him like a shaman. The patient shut his eyes, mumbled something, and took a mouthful. 'Aaah!' he gasped, passing it on, wiping the fizz from his lips. 'Aah!' said everyone in turn, straightening out at once, squaring their powerful shoulders. There would be no backache tonight.

Trying to resume our unpacking and, most pressing of all, to change into our dry clothes, I dislodged the sealed bag of picture-postcards of the Queen on horseback, Trooping the Colour. An idea presented itself: the Sovereign would save me from undue scrutiny in the transition between pairs of trousers.

'Look,' I said, 'this is for you. Here is our Tuai Rumah, our chief in England.'

'Inglang!' said the children. The cards were sheeny and metallic, the kind that change the position of their subjects as their own position is changed against the light.

I gave one to a little boy. He looked at it with amazed delight: he turned it this way and that; he scratched it and waited to see what would happen; he whipped it over, to catch a glimpse of Her Majesty from the back. Small hands thrust up like a clump of bamboo; the old woman, annoyed, demanded a pile for herself. If the children had one each, the men wanted more than one each. In five minutes, four hundred mementoes of the Empire disappeared.

There were now so many people in the room that I really wanted a photograph: with, I imagined, great stealth, I held a Fuji to my stomach, pointed it in the right direction, looked the other way myself, and pressed the button. Chaos ensued. Children howled, the women pulled their sarongs over their breasts, the men looked annoyed.

'Quick, quick – get the Polaroid,' hissed James.

With an elaborate enactment of deep apology, followed by circus gestures promising fun to come, great tricks, something quite different, and not at all offensive, I drew out the Polaroid and loaded it. The grey box would take away their image, I tried to suggest with both hands, and then give it back again. They looked dubious. I had behaved badly once, and was not really to be trusted.

The Polaroid flashed; we waited; the box whirred; the tray slid forward and proffered its wet card. I laid it on the floor, waving their fingers away. Slowly, it grew colours, like bacteria in a dish of culture. The room was very silent. They watched the outlines of heads and shoulders appear; features became defined. Suddenly they pointed to the card and to each other. Wild hilarity erupted. They clapped and clapped. They ran off to change into their best clothes and we, at last, put on our dry trousers. Only the old woman was left to grimace in astonishment, or disgust, at the whiteness, or the hairiness, of our legs.

Proudly wearing garish sarongs or Chinese shorts and tee-shirts which had been traded downriver in the rainy season, presumably, for turtles or deer or pig, for camphor or gutta-percha or rattan or pepper, they arranged themselves into family groups, forcing me to shuttle their images in and their pictures out, until the Polaroid grew hot and all the film was finished.

'What a lot of children everyone has,' I observed to Leon.

'No, no,' said Leon, 'the mothers and the fathers – they die. My own parents, they die too, sickness, or cutting trees, shick-shick,' said Leon, miming the curving descent of a parang blade, 'or in the river, bang heads on the rocks, or poison-fish, or in the jungle, hunting. You have cut. You have boil. Very painful. You have very good lucks to get better. Then you must be adopted. I adopted. My uncle and my aunt. Very kind peoples. Or the peoples in the bileks [rooms] next door. They must take the children.'

So these magnificent warrior-farmers, I thought, looking round at so much health and so much glowing muscle, at so many beautiful faces and breasts and smiles and jangling ear-rings, are the product of evolution by natural selection almost in its crudest sense.

The chief's son ushered everyone out of the huge room. We must be hungry, he said (we were); his mother and his sisters had cooked the monitor lizard (perhaps we were not quite that hungry). At the far end of the room there was a fire of split logs with a massive piece of ironwood for a hearth. A series of pots were suspended above it, and the smoke made its way out through a propped-open flap in the roof.

The girls left our mess-tins and plates in a circle round a piled bowl of rice and the hindquarters of the monitor lizard, and then withdrew. Dana served me a helping of tail, the last ten inches of it, or thereabouts; and the resin lamps flickered, and the sows and boars and piglets grunted and squealed on the rubbish and pig-shit below the floorboards; and the geckoes chick-chacked to each other in the roof spaces like mating sparrows; and I realised that the yellow-and-black-skinned monitor lizard tail would not disappear from my tin, as custom demanded, until I ate it myself.

'Makai! Makai!' said Dana.

The flesh was yellow and softish and smelt bad, very like the stray chunks of solid matter in the effluvia one sees in England on an unwashed pavement outside a public house late on a Saturday night. I eased it off the small vertebrae, mixed it into the sticky rice, and told myself that even this particular meal would all be over one day.

We were very tired. It was all too confusing; the river seemed to have spun cat's-cradles of pain out of all the muscle fibres in my calves and back; and the monitor-lizard's tail was still gently whisking, from side to side, in my stomach. I took a long pull at the arak-can and lay down on the floor of the chief's room. The huge cross-beams of the roof bucked and twisted and stuck fast on some celestial river floating over my head: I fell asleep.

'Come on,' shouted James, from a bank far away to my right, 'get up! There's going to be a welcome party.'

Staggering out, wanting to sleep as never before, I looked around, and wished I was somewhere else. The gallery was packed. The lamps had been lit. Tuak was being drunk. A long, uninviting space had been cleared in front of part of the line of longhouse doors; and around its three sides sat an expectant audience.

Leon and Inghai, looking fresh and eager, beckoned us to the back row. Dana was nowhere to be seen. He was, as Leon explained, as befitted his high and kingly status, drinking with the deputy chief of all the Kenyah on the Baleh, and was not to be disturbed, because, being Absolute Chief of all the Iban of Kapit District, he had many cares, and would soon be taking a sleeps.

We were given a glass of tuak. A tray of huge cone-shaped cheroots of Kenyah tobacco wrapped in leaves and each tied with a bow of leaf-strips was passed round; a sinuous young girl put ours in our mouths and lit them with a taper. I noticed that Leon was wearing his large and flashy, supposedly water-proof, digital watch. After its first celebratory dive with Leon into the depths of the Rajang this watch had ceased to tell the time, but it would still, if shaken violently enough, and to Leon's unvarying delight, sound its alarm.

The musicians sat in front of us. An old man held a keluri, a dried gourd shaped like a chemical retort but held upwards, and with six bamboo pipes project-ing in a bundle from its bulb; a group of young men sat ready with a bamboo harp (a tube of bamboo with raised strips cut from its surface), a bamboo xylo-phone, a bamboo flute, and a single-stringed instru-ment, a dugout-canoe-like sounding box carved from a single block of wood, the string so heavy it had to be pulled with an iron hook.

The chief's son entered, transformed. On his head he wore a war-helmet, a woven rattan cap set with black and yellow and crimson beads, topped with six long black and white plumes from the tail of the Helmeted hornbill. He was dressed in a war-coat, made from the skin of the largest cat in Borneo, the Clouded leopard. His head placed through an opening at the front of the skin, the bulk stretched down his back, and on to it were fastened row upon row of Rhinoceros hornbill feathers. Around his waist, slung on a silver belt and sheathed in a silver scabbard, was a parang to outshine all other parangs, its hilt intricately carved in horn from the antler of the kijang, the big Borneo deer. In his left hand, his arm crooked behind it, he carried a long shield, pointed at both ends, and from the centre of which a huge mask regarded us implacably, its eyes red, its teeth the painted tusks of the wild boar. Thick black tufts of hair hung in neat lines down either edge and across the top and bottom, tufts of hair which, we were led to believe, had long ago been taken from the scalps of heads cut off in battle.

Laying the ancient, and presumably fragile, shield carefully against the wall, the warrior took up his position at the centre of the floor. He crouched down and, at a nod from the man on the base string, a hollow, complicated, urgent, rhythmic music began. With exaggerated movements, his thigh muscles bunching and loosening, his tendons taut, a fierce concentration on his face, the chief's son turned slowly in time with the music, first on one foot and then on another, rising, inch by inch, to his own height, apparently peering over some imaginary cover. Sighting the enemy, he crouched again, and then, as the music quickened, he drew his bright parang and leapt violently forward, weaving and dodging, with immense exertion, cutting and striking, parrying unseen blows with his mimed shield. For a small second, his ghostly foe was off-guard, tripped on the shingle, and the heir to the Lordship of all the Kenyah of Nanga Sinyut claimed his victory with one malicious blow.

Everyone clapped and cheered, and so did I. Five young girls rushed forward to take off the hero's hornbill helmet, and war-coat, and parang. It was wonderful. The girls were very beautiful. All was right with the world. And then I realised, as a Rajah Brooke's birdwing took a flap around my duodenum, that the beautiful girls, in a troop, were coming, watched by all the longhouse, for me.

'You'll be all right,' said James, full of tuak. 'Just do your thing. Whatever it is.'

Strapped into the war-coat and the parang, the hornbill feathers on my head, I had a good idea. It would be a simple procedure to copy the basic steps that the chief's son had just shown us. There really was not much to it, after all. The music struck up, sounding just a little bit stranger than it had before.

I began the slow crouch on one leg, turning slightly. Perhaps, actually, this was a mistake, I decided. Ghastly pains ran up my thighs. Terminal cramp hit both buttocks at once. Some silly girl began to titter. A paraplegic wobble spread down my back. The silly girl began to laugh. Very slowly, the floor came up to say hello, and I lay down on it. There was uproar in the longhouse. How very funny, indeed.

Standing up, I reasoned that phase two would be easier. Peering over the imaginary boulder, I found myself looking straight into the eyes of an old man on the far side of the verandah. The old fool was crying with laughter, his ridiculous long ears waggling about. Drawing the parang, which was so badly aligned that it stuck in the belt and nearly took my fingers off, I advanced upon the foe, jumping this way and that, feeling dangerous. The old man fell off his seat. There was so much misplaced mirth, so much plain howling, that I could not hear the music, and so perhaps my rhythm was not quite right.

'Redsi!' came an unmistakable shout, 'why don't you improvise?'

Stabbed in the back just as I was about to take my very first head, I spun round violently to glare at the Fenton. I never actually saw him, because the cord of the war-helmet, not used to such movements, slipped up over the back of my head, and the helmet itself, flying forward, jammed fast over my face. Involuntarily, I took a deep gasp of its sweat-smooth rattan interior, of the hair of generations of Kenyah warriors who had each been desperate to impress the girls of their choice. It was an old and acrid smell.

The boards were shaking. The audience was out of control. And then, just in time, before suffocation set in, the five girls, grossly amused, set me free.

'Go and get James,' I spluttered, 'you go and get James.'

'Now you sing song,' shouted Leon.

'No, no – James sing songs.'

'Jams!' shouted Leon, remembering his mission.

'Jams!' The longhouse reverberated. 'Jams! Jams!' Leon had done his work well.

With great theatrical presence, offering almost no resistance to the five young girls, James processed on to the stage. The Kenyah fell silent. T. D. Freeman, in his work on Iban augury, tells us that the King of the Gods, Singalang Burong, may well be encountered in dreams. There is no mistaking him. He is almost as old as the trees, awe-inspiring, massive of body, and, a characteristic which puts his identity beyond doubt, completely bald. Judging by the slightly uneasy, deferential, expectant faces around me, Bali Penyalong, the High God of the Kenyah, was but a different name for the same deity.

The attendants withdrew. James, resplendent in leopard skin and hornbill feathers, looked even more solemn than is his habit. With the accumulated experience of many thousands of evenings at the theatre, of years of drama criticism, he regarded his audience; his huge brown eyes appeared to fix on everyone in turn. There was some backward shuffling in the front row. A dog whimpered.

The music began, a little shakily. James, in time with the music, began to mime. He was hunting something, in a perfunctory way; he made rootling movements with his head, and grunted. He was hunting a pig. Evidently successful, he butchered his quarry, selected the joint he had in mind, hung the carcase from a hook in the roof and betook himself to his ideal kitchen. Passion entered the show; James began to concentrate; his gestures quickened and the mesmerised musicians increased their tempo. He scored the pork; he basted it; he tied it with string; he made extraordinarily complex sauces; he cooked potatoes and sprouts and peas and beans and broccoli and *zucchini*, I think, until they were *fritti*. After many a tasting and many an alchemical manoeuvre with a *batterie de cuisine* decidedly better than Magny's, James deemed the gravy to be perfect. The apple sauce was plentiful. The decanted Burgundy was poured into a glass. James looked fondly at his creation and began to eat. The crackling crackled between his teeth. The warriors of the Kenyah, as if they had been present at a feast of the Gods, rose to their feet and burped. Everybody cheered.

'Jams very hungry,' said Leon to me confidentially, 'he must eat more rices.'

James held up a hand. Everyone sat down again, cross-legged.

'And now,' he announced, 'we will have a sing-song.'

'Inglang song! Inglang song!' shouted Inghai, wildly excited, and full of arak.

And then James really did astonish me. To the beat of the big string he launched into a rhyming ballad, a long spontaneous poem about our coming from a far country, entering the Rajang from the sea, about the pleasures of the Baleh and the danger of the rapids and the hospitality of the strongest, the most beautiful people in all the world, the Kenyah of Nanga Sinyut.

I clapped as wildly as Inghai. 'Bravo Jams!' I shouted; 'Bravo Jams!' mimicked Inghai; 'Bravo! Bravo!' sang the Kenyah.

James indicated that he was tired; he pillowed his black-and-white-plumed head on his hands. But it was no use. We wanted more songs. We wanted so many, in fact, that I discovered, to my amazement, that he knew almost every popular and music-hall song back to about 1910 and that he could adapt their tunes to the vagaries of the bamboo gourd-pipes with professional ease.

James was saved, just before he collapsed from exhaustion, when the longhouse clown stood up, jealous of his great success. The helmet and coat were laid aside, and James sat down. But my annoyance was short-lived. People began to laugh before the clown had done anything at all, and it soon became obvious that he was a very witty Fool indeed.

With exaggerated seriousness, he sat on the floor, his legs outstretched; he put on an imaginary hat and he fastened his imaginary shirt-cuffs. He looked about, unconcerned, like a great chief.

'It's Jams!' said Leon, 'It's Jams in the boat! He very serious man!'

'Jams!' said the Kenyah, laughing with recognition and approval.

The clown then got out of the longboat and became a Neandethaler, struggling in the river, pulling the dugout this way and that, always getting it wrong, unable to walk and push at the same time, his movements constantly directed, with a frantic exasperation of contradictory gestures, by Dana and Leon and Inghai. There were roars of laughter.

'It's Redmon!' said Leon. 'He very fats!'

The chief's son then stood up and announced something. The long gallery became quiet again. He pointed to about fifteen men, in turn, who followed him on to the floor. They were all young and eager, bodily alert, absurdly fit. Long-backed, with fairly short, lavishly muscled limbs, they looked like athletes at the peak of their careers, assembling at the Olympics for the men's pentathlon.

'They all bachelors,' whispered Leon. 'They not yet picked their womens.'

The men formed into a single line, by order of height. And a completely different kind of music began, violent, aggressive, with a menacing and insistent beat. They walked slowly forward, unsmiling, stamping their feet, looking rhythmically to either side, intent. This, I realised, was the dance described in Hose, albeit the protagonists were wearing shorts and singlets:

The bigger boys are taught to take part in the dance in which the return from the warpath is dramatically represented.

This is a musical march rather than a dance. A party of young men in full war-dress form up in single line; the leader, and perhaps two or three others, play the battle march on the *keluri*. The line advances slowly up the gallery, each man turning half about at every third step, the even numbers turning to the one hand, the odd to the other hand, alternately, and all stamping together as they complete the turn at each third step. The turning to right and left symbolises the alert guarding of the heads which are supposed to be carried by the victorious warriors.

After five march-pasts, as I was deciding that this would not be a sensible longhouse to attack even if one really was in the SAS, everyone relaxed, and we were invited to join the line. James picked up the rhythm at once, but I found even these steps difficult, falling over my boots. All the girls giggled.

'Redmon,' said Leon, when we sat down again, 'you so big, your feet too far from your head.'

'That's it. That's exactly what it is.'

There was a pause.

'Or, maybe,' said Leon, 'you so fats you can't see them.'

Leon, with gross bad manners, uncrossed his legs, lay flat out on the floor, and laughed at his own joke, re-directing his attention, sharply, only when the unmarried girls stood up.

Gracefully, shyly, the young girls aligned themselves.

'Look at that one,' said Leon, 'look at that one in the pink sarong. Redmon. Just *look* at that one.'

'Behave yourself,' I said, testily. 'This is no time for one of your jumps. You'll get us all killed.'

'She the moon in the sky,' said Leon.

The girls, to a delicate, lilting dance-tune, began their own movement across the long stage and back again; lithe, slender, very young, they were indeed lovely to look at; and their dance was deliciously fragile after the violence of the men. With small, flowing movements of their wrists and fingers, all in synchrony, their arms rippling, their supple bodies undulating slightly, they mimicked the leisurely flight of the hornbill. The forward step on the beat outlined the legs beneath their folded-down sarongs. The gentle, backward swaying, on the pause, revealed the tight breasts beneath their tee-shirts.

Leon's eyes were wide, as wide as they had been when he shot his turtle. I blew in his ear.

'Shush,' said Leon. 'You be quiets. Now we watch.'

Looking round to poke Inghai, I saw that he was asleep, curled up on the floor, still holding his arak mug in both hands. All the men were very quiet.

Far too soon, the dance was over. We clapped, adoringly, sentimentally, soppily, feeling a little weak. The girls, blushing, scurried to their seats and giggled. But the girl in the pink sarong returned, carrying two huge bunches of hornbill feathers. They were strapped to her wrists, set out and fixed like an open fan. Her features were strikingly beautiful, certainly; her hair, about a foot longer than that of the other girls, was combed down, loose and fine, black and silky, to her waist. Her looped ear-lobes, weighted with rings, hung down only to the base of her smooth neck, soft and brown in the light of the lamp. The tattoos on her arms were only half-complete and, as tattooing begins in a girl's tenth year and continues in small bouts at regular intervals (otherwise the pain of the operation would be insupportable and the ensuing inflammation probably fatal), she could be, I calculated, no more than fourteen or fifteen years old.

'Leon,' I said, 'she's far too young. She's only fourteen.'

'What is it?' said Leon. 'What is it? You sit stills. You be quiets. Now we watch.'

However young, she danced with tremulous invitation, a slow, yearning, graceful dance, the long fan feathers sweeping over her body in alternating curves, a dance that began from a crouching position and opened gradually upwards as she rose, inch by inch, a celestial bird, some as-yet-undiscovered hornbill of paradise, flying upwards towards the sun, towards the bright world where Bali Penyalong is Lord of the House.

'This is really something,' whispered James, holding his head in both hands, gazing at her. And then, perhaps remembering his professional self, his column inches, 'she *really, really* knows what she's doing.'

The two fans of the tail feathers of the Rhinoceros hornbill, at the end of her outstretched arms, joined above her head. She stood at her full height, little, curved, lissome, beautiful. We clapped and clapped.

And then, suddenly looking straight at us, giving us a small charge of our own internal electricity, a conger eel uncurling in the guts, she walked into the audience with every eye upon her and pulled Leon to his feet.

Leon's brown face grew browner and browner. He was blushing. He was suffusing, uncontrollably, with blood, and surprise, with fright and pride, with increasing vigour and overpowering lust.

She tied him, very slowly, into the helmet and the war-coat, lingering over every knot, staring steadily into his eyes, hanging the belt around his waist with both her hands, arranging the silver parang so that it hung neatly down the outside of his right thigh.

Leon, taller and darker than the Kenyah, and just as fit, stood like a warrior; and this was his reward, I realised. For Leon, conqueror of the river, as she must have heard, had proved his manhood and his spontaneous, natural courage as surely as if he had arrived at Nanga Sinyut with a severed head. In our eyes, and probably in theirs, he had done much better: he had saved one, and a particularly fine specimen, too, a Bald godhead rescued from a blow amongst the rocks.

Still fired with inspiration, his face growing even darker, he nodded to his little muse in lordly fashion as she returned to her seat. He then, I am sure, executed the finest dance of his life. To the frantic music of open combat, he somersaulted backwards; he cartwheeled from side to side; he cut heads like corn; he lunged and feinted and dodged behind his imaginary shield; he twisted and spun through the air faster than flying spears. For his new love, he topped whole armies. He moved with such energy that black and white banded wheels, images of hornbill feathers, arcs and lines, seemed to hang in the murk all around him, fading and appearing in the flicker of the lamp.

Finally, the music stopped and Leon, shiny with sweat and grasping, I assume, a bundle of heads, strode with them to the side of his beloved and dropped them in her lap. In the stunned, short pause before the clapping began I heard an odd noise. It was not a gecko. It was Leon's watch. It was as shaken and over-excited as he was. *Beeeep-beeeep-beeeep* it said.

Leon, disrobed, momentarily speechless with exertion and wanting a rest, woke up Inghai with his foot. Ingy-Pingy, bleary but goodnatured, not at all sure where he was, did the kind of kung-fu which a dormouse might do, on arising from hibernation. He yawned and uncurled and stretched his arms and legs full out a bit, and then went back to sleep.

The formal gathering broke up into small groups, drinking and laughing and telling stories. The largest circle grew around James. The Kenyah sat at his feet in rings, listening to his bizarre tales of life in England.

They studied his expressive face and his agitated gestures, laughing at the right moments, tingling, when required, at the voice from the Hammer House of Horror, just as if they knew where Rugeley was, or were connoisseurs of murder, or understood two words of what he said.

Maybe the arak and tuak were beginning to tell on me. My legs seemed to have contracted elephantiasis. It was difficult to focus. The longhouse pitched a bit, like an anchored canoe. Or maybe I was simply coming to the end of the longest day I ever hope to traverse.

As if from a long way off, I heard James issue a solemn warning to his audience:

> The Butcher bird, or Red-backed shrike
> Should not be trusted with your bike
> The pump and light he whips away
> And takes the spokes to spike his prey.

It was an entirely new, unpublished Fenton poem, I realised, dimly. But whatever it was, it was beyond me. And so were the Kenyah. I staggered, luckily, the right way off the verandah, through the correct bilek door, and found my patch of board. Through the wooden wall I could hear James singing songs, parcelling out the verses, teaching the Kenyah English. I fell asleep.

POCKET PENGUINS

36. **Muriel Spark** The Snobs
37. **Steven Pinker** Hotheads
38. **Tony Harrison** Under the Clock
39. **John Updike** Three Trips
40. **Will Self** Design Faults in the Volvo 760 Turbo
41. **H. G. Wells** The Country of the Blind
42. **Noam Chomsky** Doctrines and Visions
43. **Jamie Oliver** Something for the Weekend
44. **Virginia Woolf** Street Haunting
45. **Zadie Smith** Martha and Hanwell
46. **John Mortimer** The Scales of Justice
47. **F. Scott Fitzgerald** The Diamond as Big as the Ritz
48. **Roger McGough** The State of Poetry
49. **Ian Kershaw** Death in the Bunker
50. **Gabriel García Márquez** Seventeen Poisoned Englishmen
51. **Steven Runciman** The Assault on Jerusalem
52. **Sue Townsend** The Queen in Hell Close
53. **Primo Levi** Iron Potassium Nickel
54. **Alistair Cooke** Letters from Four Seasons
55. **William Boyd** Protobiography
56. **Robert Graves** Caligula
57. **Melissa Bank** The Worst Thing a Suburban Girl Could Imagine
58. **Truman Capote** My Side of the Matter
59. **David Lodge** Scenes of Academic Life
60. **Anton Chekhov** The Kiss
61. **Claire Tomalin** Young Bysshe
62. **David Cannadine** The Aristocratic Adventurer
63. **P. G. Wodehouse** Jeeves and the Impending Doom
64. **Franz Kafka** The Great Wall of China
65. **Dave Eggers** Short Short Stories
66. **Evelyn Waugh** The Coronation of Haile Selassie
67. **Pat Barker** War Talk
68. **Jonathan Coe** 9th & 13th
69. **John Steinbeck** Murder
70. **Alain de Botton** On Seeing and Noticing